The Doctor Has the Flu

Written by Carolyn Clark   Illustrated by Daniel Vasconcellos

Oh, no! The doctor has the flu!
We told Dad just what to do.

3

Stay in bed and eat some fruit.

4

Hold your nose and play the flute.

5

Hum a tune just for fun.

Run a race in the sun.

Chew some gum and make some stew.

Add three bugs and a shoe.

9

Then jump up and down on the bed.

10

Put a moose on your head.

Jump onto a big blue truck.

Play a game with a duck.

Trust us. We know what to do.
Soon you'll be as good as new.

What great help. You've done your best.

Now you all need to rest.